Priority Focused Finances
Align to what really matters

Ann Holman

© 2020 Ann Holman

All rights reserved. No part of this book may be reproduced, stored in a retrieval system, or transmitted in any form or by any means – electronic, mechanical, photocopy, recording, scanning, or other – except for brief quotations in critical reviews or articles, without the prior written permission of the publisher.

In some instances, names, dates, locations, and other identifying details have been changed to protect the identities and privacy of those mentioned in this book.

Legal & Disclaimer

The information contained in this book is not designed to replace or take the place of any form of medicine or professional medical or financial advice. The information in this book has been provided for educational and entertainment purposes only.

The information contained in this book has been compiled from sources deemed reliable, and it is accurate to the best of the Author's knowledge; however, the Author cannot guarantee its accuracy and validity and cannot be held liable for any errors or omissions. Changes are periodically made to this book. You must consult your doctor or financial specialist before using any of the suggested remedies, techniques, or information in this book.

Upon using the information contained in this book, you agree to hold harmless the Author from and against any damages, costs, and expenses, including any legal fees potentially resulting from the application of any of the information provided by this guide. This disclaimer applies to any damages or injury caused by the use and application, whether directly or indirectly, of any advice or information presented, whether for breach of contract, tort, negligence, personal injury or financial consequences, criminal intent, or under any other cause of action.

You agree to accept all risks of using the information presented inside this book.

This is dedicated to everyone who helped me answer the question,

"How can I stop living paycheck-to-paycheck?"

and especially the ones who helped me
when I didn't even know what questions to ask.

Thank you, ET2 Jones, for noticing that I desperately needed help.

Table of Contents

Introduction	
Pre-Work	page 1
What Exactly ARE Your Priorities?	Page 9
Priority-Focused Financial Policies	page 17
Bills and Expenses	page 25
Bills and Expenses Hacks	page 29
Respecting Income Sources	page 33
The Emergency Fund	page 43
Ready For A Budget?	Page 49
The Priority-Focused Budget	page 53
The Pay-Yourself-First Method	page 55
Irregular or Insufficient Pay Periods	page 57
The Debts	page 67
Income Emergency Fund	page 73
You Did It!	Page 79
Frequently Asked Questions	page 85
Wrap Up	page 91
Recommended Reading	page 93

Introduction

I am so excited about this book! As much as I loved teaching this content in an online course and the one-on-one time with my students, I love the reach of a simple book. There are no scheduling and distance constraints to learning from a book. And for some, there's also not a cost constraint. That brings my heart joy.

And I'm equally excited for you! That you are not only choosing to read this book, but are going to put in the time and effort to apply these steps, simple but not easy, in order to propel your financial life in the direction that you know is right for you.

The way this book will work is that in many of the chapters there will be action expected of you. Whether it's to figure out your debts, or to prioritize which income strategies you will try out. Don't be afraid to actually DO these actions, as it is through our actions that we gain the results we desire.

There is also a Priority Focused Finances Monthly Journal! https://amzn.to/3emJe97. It's a great place to write out the things you learn in this book!

And without further ado, let's get to the pre-work!

Pre-Work

What is this pre-work? Well, with any issue, we must first take stock of where we are.

If we are unhappy with our relationships, we should assess those relationships first, before we come up with how to help them out. If we are feeling ill, we must first be able to describe the symptoms before we can expect a doctor to provide a prescription.

And it's the same with our finances.

So let's check out the situation, see where we are at, so that we know the lay of the land today, and then we will figure out the direction we want to head tomorrow.

Webster's dictionary defines *budget* as, "a statement of estimated income and expenses for a period of time," or a "plan for using money."

There's a belief that people who have a budget may be financially constrained: they're the "bargain hunters", "budget travelers", they "love a good deal" and always "pay the least amount possible".

And while that is sometimes true, let's get back to the definition: it's just a plan for using your money.

A budget is not necessarily about being a penny-pincher or limiting your expenses (although it can be), but it is about making a plan for where your money will go.

And who gets to make that plan? You.

Just you. Not your parents, friends, children, the media, any celebrities, or me.

It's you. All you. Now for some, that's super intimidating. Being the one in charge of finances (especially for a family) can be quite daunting, but don't worry: We're going to break it down. And you may be surprised to find that there are different WAYS to budget, and not all of them even include the traditional, income-minus-expenses concepts.

But before we fully dive in, we've got to do some pre-work. And just know this: the numbers you are about to track down will NOT stay this way. These numbers are more fluid than you think. But we've got to have a starting point, so let's start here.

Income Assignment.

Assignment number one is to figure out how much money you've got coming in.

Don't just think about the obvious sources. Of course I want you to mention your job, including how much you get paid, how frequently, and whether it varies. If it varies, then write the lowest and highest amounts, and it could help to make a note on what contributes to the variation. Maybe it is commissions-dependent, maybe your work hours vary, et cetera.

But don't forget all the other ways that you make money. Examples are babysitting, dog-walking, selling things on Facebook marketplace, heck I want to know if there's been a reliable amount you've made in tax returns each year, everything.
And as a bonus, you could even mention the non-monetary income that you may have. Probably more accurate to refer to these as "resources."
Does someone watch your children for free while you work? That's a huge resource.
Does your sister give you all her children's outgrown clothing for your child? Another huge resource.
The benefit of writing these resources down is to get your mind thinking outside the box. Sometimes it is our resourcefulness that help out our budget more than our "income."
Nothing is extra; it all counts.

After you've written down how much money or resources you've got coming in, it helps to end with some gratitude. Gratitude that you have income and other resources coming in; gratitude that these numbers are flexible and can always increase (or decrease, especially if it's tied to a task/job that you hate!); gratitude that there are so many different ways to make a living and have income that we couldn't possibly even write a book on it (although we'll give some more examples later!).

Debt Assignment

Okay, you already know what to do! Write down those debts.

Not what your bills are, (that's next) but your debts: money you owe, how much you owe, to whom do you owe it, and is there a pre-agreed-upon payment plan (example: minimum monthly payments on your loans).

And just as it was helpful to write down your resources as part of your income, it's also helpful to write down the resources you provide to others! Are there obligations that you are fulfilling and that you are most likely to continue fulfilling? Let's write those down, too.
Our time and skills are as precious, if not more, than our monetary assets. Let's see where those are going. You don't need to get in the weeds with these resources, but take a moment to at least reflect on them.

On the monetary side, this includes all loans, from mortgage and car to personal, student, and credit cards. And if you owe your mom $20, I want you to write that down, too.

Significant or not, write them out.
And let's end with some gratitude!

Now there's a part of us that may resent when we owe money (and resent when we owe someone our time). We resent having student loans that take eons to pay off, we regret the poor decisions that lead to credit card debt, or the car that's too expensive, or the house that's too big! We may even resent the hours of our life that we are "giving away" to our employers, or to other organizations or even people.

But let's take a moment today to thank our debts, both monetary and time-related. We need to be grateful that whenever that debt was created, we were afforded the opportunity to try something that we couldn't otherwise afford. That we have experiences that will be a building block to future, higher-quality experiences (like being debt free AND living the life of our dreams).

We needed those experiences, and yes, that debt, to become the person we are today. And that person is amazing, and clearly seeking to grow into an even more awesome person!

So thank you, $300 credit card debt that took me four years to pay off... I needed to learn that buying a suede leather jacket doesn't really make me happy.

Bills Assignment

This is the part that most people dread, but don't worry - we've got this. It's the bills.

You already know how much money is coming in, and how much you owe.

Now you're going to break your bills down into three parts:

Part 1: Minimum payments.
This first part is easy because you already did most of it and that is knowing your minimum payments for your debts. Write the amount and actual date the payment is due. For example, if your car payment is due on the third of the month, write that down.

For debts that don't have a payment plan, just write down how much you owe again. If you owe your mom $2,000 but she didn't give you a payment plan requirement, write down the $2,000, but put a little asterisk (*) beside it because you're going to figure out your own payment plan. This is super nice because you can make it fit within the entire budget!

For debts that have a delayed payment, still write the payment amount and the dates. For example, if you get a year before payments kick in, write down what the payments will be, and the date it starts, so if you'll be paying $300 a month starting in six months, write that down and be specific (eg. the 15th of December, 2021).

Part 2: Obligatory bills.
This includes your utilities, cellphone bill, insurance, dance classes, Netflix, Amazon Prime membership, any subscriptions, et cetera.

Anything that is a set bill, that you know you will pay for. Perhaps it's even withdrawn automatically.

Again, write down the dollar amount (for variables, write the lowest and highest amounts), the actual date it's due, and note that some bills are every four weeks versus monthly, while others are annual or semi-annual so it will be helpful to write down the exact dates they are due in the next few payments.

Part 3: Recurring life expenses.

Lastly, flexible and recurring life expenses. This is where your groceries come in (and if you added it under obligatory, that's completely fine!), your car gas, Starbucks habit, your weekly girls night out expenses, your monthly manicures, et cetera. Again, lowest to highest with a note on why it might be higher or why the frequency may change.

For this part, don't overthink it. You can, of course, look at recent bank statements to confirm your habits, or you could simply guestimate, and over time you'll see how realistic your numbers truly are, and you will adjust your budget as needed.

That's the beauty of a budget. It's a living budget, it can be adjusted! Each month or each pay period is never the exact same - and that's fine. We're here to navigate how to make this work. So for now, write what you can - and we'll get it to be more accurate later.

And as always, let's thank our bills! If it wasn't for these bills, we couldn't drive to the places we need or want to go, we couldn't have our home, we couldn't be sociable or take yoga classes. Let's be grateful that we are able to do the things we want to do!

What Exactly ARE Your Priorities?

If I were to sum up the concept of this entire course into one chapter, this would be it. This is where you hone in on your priority, your purpose, your joy. This is the step that too many people miss, not just with their finances, but in life!

I've been doing this, in some variation or format, pretty much my entire life. This is where my confidence comes from in all my decisions.

This is the key to knowing what "right" looks like for YOU, and very often it is extremely different from what right looks like for anyone else.

Don't skip this step.

Before we begin, there are some things you're going to need for this chapter. Take a moment to find some paper or a notebook, and something to write with. You could also use the Priority Focused Finances Monthly Journal, specially designed for this exercise and more! https://amzn.to/3emJe97 You're not doing a penmanship exercise, so don't be afraid to use a pen. Sometimes when you're free-flow writing, the truth comes out, and you don't want to be tempted to delete those initial words. Striking a line through your written words so you can still read your initial gut writing is helpful, even if you revise it to something more effective.

While I will focus a bit more on the financial portions, I just want to stress the relevance this exercise has to all areas of your life. Because isn't the purpose of having financial priorities really about all the other priorities? Would there really be a point in a budget if you didn't know what matters to you?

And did I mention you need to get some paper and a pen? Did you get it yet? Why don't you do that now [Said in my "mom voice"... sounds like a question but it isn't]. We're not going to just think about it, we're going to write it. There's magic in words. There's magic in the act of writing things out.

Let's begin.

I'm going to give you two areas of finance, and what I want you to do is write at least two to three sentences describing what would make that area a "perfect 10" if you were to score that in your life.
If you had zero headaches or negative stress in each of those areas, what would that look like? How would you feel, how involved would you be?

This is where you lean into **you**.

Don't think about what your family wants for you. Don't think about what your spouse/partner would want, or your children, your co-workers, or friends. Don't even think about what you imagine Dave Ramsey, Jordan Paige or any finance guru might recommend. **You** are the only one that matters right now.

First Financial Area: Your Budget

What would perfect look like in this financial area if everything were aligned?

Where and how much money would be coming in, how much would be going out, and what would it go towards?

How do you want to feel about your budget? How do you want to feel about how you spend money on a daily, weekly, monthly basis? What does perfect look like for your budget? Do you even want to have a "traditional" budget?

You don't have to answer these specific questions, I'm just giving some context for what this area entails.

Second Financial Area: Investments

How do you want to feel and how involved do you want to be in the area of investments? Unlike your budget, which is where your money will go today, this is how you want to feel about the money you put aside, perhaps in savings, or other accounts where it is invested in some manner, to provide for your future. This includes how much debt you are comfortable with, if at all. What does a "perfect 10" look like in regards to investments and your financial future? What do you want to save for? What are the future concerns that you want to feel confident about today?

Would you want your investments to also support other people or organizations?

Again, you don't have to answer these questions in particular... just focus on investments.

The other areas.

If you want to dive deeper, you can explore the non-financial areas. Remember that the purpose of your finances, ultimately, is to fund these other areas, so they matter just as much (if not more) than the financial areas. Life isn't just about money; **you** aren't just about the money.

Let's honor the different aspects of our lives by giving them a closer look! Describe what a "perfect 10" would look like in each of these areas of your life. Envision what your priorities are, what are the things that matter to you. I'm going to give you a list to work from, and you can feel free to add or adapt the categories.

First Health Area: Mental, emotional, psychological health.
Second Health Area: Physical abilities.
Third Health Area: Nutritional health.

First Relationship Area: Spirituality, Godly relationships.
Second Relationship Area: Family relationships.
Third Relationship Area: Social relationships

First Personal Area: Hobbies you enjoy spending time doing.
Second Personal Area: Personal development, or education.
Third Personal Area: Your environment

First Career Area: Current career.
Second Career Area: Future or dream career.
Third Career Area: Side hustles or passive incomes.

This is an exercise that you should complete every three to six months because our lives change. You don't have to complete it for every area. This quarter you might feel pulled to work on your relationships, next quarter you may realize that your health needs maximum attention.

We evolve, we mature, we gain experience and awareness over time. Your priorities as a 12-year-old are surely not what they are as a 30-year-old and if you ever focus on personal development, you'll find that your priorities as a 30 year-old can be dramatically different from your priorities as a 31 year-old.

Once you are done filling each of these categories in, do a once over. Sometimes your priorities in one area can actually conflict with another area. It's important to take some time, close your eyes if it helps, and dream about how it would look for ALL of these individual areas to align. What would a typical day look like if these things were indeed true. If you want to be a body builder, putting 10 hours a day towards achieving this, how would that align with your desire to homeschool your children or to become the next President of the United States? I'm not suggesting that these three things are impossible... only that for it to become a reality, you must first be able to see it happening.

Sometimes in certain areas we have a "dream" or a preconceived notion of how things "should" be, but when we align it to all of our other dreams, we see which ones have higher priorities for us.

As an example, some days (especially when I read a lot about becoming a vegetarian and all the physical and emotional benefits to that lifestyle) I imagine that I want to become a vegan. But that conflicts with my very specific dreams about traveling the world with my son and eating literally ALL of the amazing cultural foods that exist... the majority of which are decidedly NOT vegan. If you know me at all, you know that travel and spontaneously eating something I've never had before is something I seriously love! So while I may one day try out the vegan lifestyle, it's simply not for me right now. It doesn't align yet.

You will know what is right for you when you realize that some priorities contradict what you just wrote in other priority categories. You will know which opportunities are FOR you and which are NOT, by taking a moment to envision your typical, "perfect 10" day.

We all have a purpose, we were all made to live in our purpose. And while it's sometimes difficult to know what that purpose is, if you lean into the things that make you feel right, the things that make you happy, you'll find your purpose is absolutely related to how you want to feel and what a perfect 10 looks like for you. And once you know what perfect looks like, once you know the trajectory of your life, once you know the direction that you want to go towards, the choices, the decisions get so much easier.

We were not created to "be like everybody else" or to worry about "everything". We need to divide and conquer to make the world a better place - and if we each lean into our own heart, we will know where and how to contribute.

Note: For those of you with a spouse or partner, or children that you want involved in the creation of your lives, it's a good idea to both do this individually first. After you have done it separately, then come together and compare and contrast to find where the balances can be made.

Figure out what areas you can work on together and in what areas you'll be flying solo. Yes, compromises may be necessary, but we've got to know where we're starting from before we discuss compromises and how to distribute the financial and decision-making responsibilities.

The beauty of having a partner whose vision of perfect isn't 100% in alignment with yours is that your life will probably mature in more unexpected and beautiful ways. Don't be afraid of being different. Lean into this as well.

Priority-Focused Financial Policies

One of my favorite Bible verses is 1 Corinthians 14:33: "God is not the author of confusion."

Clarity not only makes life so much more enjoyable, but it makes our dreams possible.

We're gonna take the priorities we already identified in the last chapter and create clear policies that support them. Taking those vague concepts that we wrote down as our priorities and creating policies makes them much more specific, much more actionable, so that we can actually accomplish something, we can actually create our dreams.

It's one thing to say "I want to eat healthier" and another thing to write down what that means. What specifically are you going to buy? What are you going to avoid buying? The more specific (and realistic), the easier it is when we go shopping to know exactly what you're going to get.

And while we will definitely focus on our financial priorities, this is something you can apply to all areas. What's super cool is that a policy will generally end up covering more than one priority area. So a "financial policy" can also cover a parenting priority, it can cover a health priority, an environmental priority, etc.

There are three basic rules to follow when creating a policy:

Rule #1- A policy must not, in any way, shape or form conflict with ANY of our priorities.

Rule #2- A policy must directly support at least one priority.

Rule #3- Less is more: you do not need everything to be spelled out in a policy.

Let's dive deeper into what each of these rules means.

Rule #1

Even though we're focusing on our financial priorities, it would make zero sense to create a policy that harms your relationships, or harms your future career, etc. We are multi-dimensional and we want to be respectful to all of our concerns, not just the financial. Yes, there are times when the financial burdens/concerns are such that a temporary pause on focusing on the other priorities may be valid. But there is never a need to bring harm to or negatively impact the other areas.

Rule #2

There are billions of good ideas, goals, and policies in the world - but don't get caught up in copying someone else's great ideas! We should only ever make a policy that directly supports at least one of our priorities!

For example, creating a policy that will help you to lose weight might be an amazing thing to do! But if nowhere in your priorities did you write the need/desire to lose weight, then would it make sense to create a policy that would focus on that? Of course not. These are

YOUR policies, not your favorite health coach's (and personal soap box: we, as a community, need to focus less on the scale, and more on our health!).

And also know that policies, just like priorities, do evolve over time. So it's not that you'll never focus on something that you don't have written down now, it just means that now is not that time.

Rule #3
Less is more. We just need a few policies to give us some guidelines - and it's okay if some of those policies are created later, and it's okay if we tweak a policy when we realize it's not ideal (maybe it doesn't seem to harm another priority, but we later learn that it does, then it's a good time to change it).

This is where I used to actually spell out the policies my students should make. But the thing is, it's a lot less effective when I tell you your policies, versus letting you make your own.

So rather, I will give you some sample policies to get your juices flowing. Some of these policies are ones that I created for myself, and others were created by students in my course.

"I will only let my son purchase a new toy or buy a new or upgraded app on the weekend after the 15th of the month, and I will make sure that I schedule in time to go to the store of his choice to get the item."

This policy covers budget, because the mother only had extra funds on the 15th of the month, as well as improving her relationship with her son, since this policy stopped the constant whining for new toys that would happen any time they would go to the store together. It stopped the whining when the son realized that on the 15th, his mother would make a special trip to the store ESPECIALLY to buy a new toy with him, thus making him realize that HIS happiness is a priority for her, and so he doesn't need to demand attention for it anymore. Overall, she spends less money on her son's toy collection by creating this dedicated moment for shopping, while also increasing their closeness AND teaching her son the joys of delayed gratification and budgeting.

"I will buy gas on Wednesdays no matter how much gas I have left in my car."

This policy stemmed from a lady who got paid every Friday. She found herself waiting until Friday to purchase gas, which made sense on paper, but was inconvenient because on Fridays she would often want to go for a drive somewhere but had to delay the outing to wait in what was usually a long line at her gas station. Changing it to Wednesdays meant she had to be more intentional with her budget during the week so she wouldn't run out by Friday, and it allowed her to get gas on a day when the line was non-existent at her gas station, thus making life more enjoyable in general.

"I will only use my savings account funds if it is an actual life-related emergency."

This policy is more obvious, but the creator of this policy was surprised at how often she dipped into her funds during the month and it helped her to better determine if something she wanted to purchase really was an "emergency" or just a purchase out of boredom or stress. She also increased her budget to include taking a yoga class three times a week to help her with her stress (and not only was she able to maintain her emergency fund at her preferred balance, but she was able to invest into other accounts, which she had never before managed.)

"I will go grocery shopping every Monday and Thursday."

This policy stemmed from a woman who used to do the bulk of her groceries monthly, with weekly trips, usually on the weekend, for more perishable items. Some of her challenges with monthly shopping was that she would purchase items that ultimately didn't ever cook because her eating mood would change, and so she would just go out to a restaurant instead of cooking. Even her weekly perishable items tended to go bad before she actually used them because she simply wouldn't eat them. Once she started to go shopping twice a week, she found she was more likely to actually still WANT to eat what she purchased, thereby reducing the amount of food she threw away and reducing how often she would give up and go to a restaurant. Turns out a 3-day meal plan worked more efficiently for her than a weekly or monthly plan.

"I will put aside $50 each month to go towards a birthday vacation each year."

The gentleman who made the policy was finally able to admit that his birthdays WERE special to him and that he was often disappointed in the gifts his wife and family would give him. Because he shared this policy with his wife, rather than deciding what gifts she should get him for his birthday, she instead helped him plan a birthday get-away, which he spent fishing with his friends later that year.

I will take this time to note that even though this was how he wanted to spend his birthday, his wife preferred getting a spontaneous gift from him, and so she did not put aside any funds per se, for her birthday. While some husbands and wives feel the need to spend "the same amount" on each other for their birthdays, or other holidays, we are NOT our spouses and do not need to "copy" each other.

I hope these examples will be helpful in creating your own policies. While there is nothing wrong with the traditional, "I will put all my extra funds towards paying off my credit card debt" or "I will put away $100 each month towards my savings account", there is something powerful in having a specific policy that fills not only our financial priorities, but also priorities that affect the other parts of our lives.

"I will put all my extra funds towards paying off my debts to quit my job."

"I will put away $100 each month towards my savings account so I never again have to deal with the financial trauma that I had to deal with today."

Also know that it's okay to add a policy that you will spend more on an area of your life, even if you currently have debt. Priority-focused finances is NOT about putting all your energy and efforts into your finances (although there are times in life where that is necessary.)

It is about knowing what your priorities are and making sure that your entire life reflects those priorities, to include your finances.

Bills and Expenses

When I first started focusing my budget on my priorities, I was active duty in the Navy, and only had my Navy income to rely on. We got paid twice a month, on the first and the 15th. I found this to be super irritating since most of my bills happened on the first of the month, and almost nothing on the 15th. This left me being super stressed out the first half of the month, and led to over-indulging on the second half of the month. I would often find myself still using credit cards to get me through the first two weeks, and then "promising myself" that I would pay it all back when I got my second paycheck. But since I didn't keep a close eye on penny for penny (and who likes to live that way, anyway), more often than not I would go further into debt each month, while wasting money on things that weren't really a priority for me.

This is where your priorities, which you wrote a few chapters ago, really come into play. In fact, take a moment and read through those priorities right now - to make sure they're fresh in your memory! Also read over your policies. It's always helpful.

Then as you look at your list of bills and expenses, for each item ask yourself this question:
Is this bill or expense in alignment with my priorities? It either supports your priorities or it harms your priorities. Try not to think of any expense as "neutral."

"If it's not a hell yes, it's a hell no!"

Anything you aren't happy, excited, grateful, honored, thrilled, ecstatic, and grateful to purchase or spend your money on, should be reconsidered.

I'ma say it again for the people in the back.

EVERYTHING that you're paying for should make you feel amazing and proud to purchase.

Literally everything.

And if it doesn't make you happy, you should seriously consider why you're putting your money (and probably your time and energy) towards it.

So again, is this bill or expense in alignment with your priorities? It either supports your priorities or it harms your priorities. Try not to think of any expense as "neutral."

If it's harmful, scratch that bill or expense out. It's a non-negotiable if it goes against your priorities. While some bills "may" have some type of obligation (let's say there's a minimum subscription length or an early termination fee), sometimes it's worth it to pay for the early termination. For one thing, you will avoid forgetting to cancel it before it automatically renews. Also, the amount you're paying for the termination fee may be less than another 10 months of obligatory payments (or however many payments are due). But either way, get rid of that expense.

There are some concepts that appear neutral, such as getting a bundle for internet, cable and a landline, when you don't use one or even two of the services. I would look HARD at these types of expenses, as more often than not you're still getting the short end of the deal. And look deeper than, "well, sometimes I like to watch tv." But do you really? Would you get the same joy from watching Netflix or Hulu which are often cheaper than cable? And on that note, do you really need Netflix AND Hulu AND DisneyPlus? I originally had DisneyPlus for my son, in addition to Netflix. When I asked my son if he wanted both, he was enthusiastic in his yes. When I told him that I had to get rid of one, he quickly said, "Well, don't get rid of Netflix!"

You see, as a general rule, my son is a fan of "more." But when it's put on the line, and he's told to actually get rid of something, he rarely hesitates to protect what's important to him (because he knows I'm serious and WILL get rid of something.) I saw that it was an easy decision for him and knew that getting rid of DisneyPlus was the right decision for us. Many months later and he hasn't even brought up a show that he "misses" from DisneyPlus, and when he's bored with Netflix, it turns out he has a ton of toys, books, a dog, lots of artistic choices and friends available to entertain him!

If an expense or bill is supportive of your priorities, feel free to keep that item. But again, why not do a little price-shopping? Keep in mind that quality is still very much relevant. You don't want to penny pinch on your priorities and decrease value! Very often, brand is less important, or all the frills are unnecessary. And this is where you should occasionally price-shop and do a value comparison to see if you are really getting the best quality. Also, by eliminating the harmful expenses and correcting the so-called neutral ones, you've possibly got money to play with. When it comes to priorities, it's okay to "spend more" if the quality is worth it AND if it's within your priorities! You want to do this carefully and with great consideration.

But eliminate the harmful or neutral line items quickly! Better to go without than to waste your time and money on mediocre products or experiences.

The minimum payments on debts are fairly self-explanatory, but know this: if your budget works out to where you are negative each pay period, or even one pay period, it may be worth the effort to call creditors and try and reduce your minimum payment! There are some tricks to this, in a later chapter, but for now we are going to zoom in on bills and expenses.

Bills and Expenses Hacks

I know you are really excited to learn some expense hacks!

Please note: just because I give you some hacks in a particular category, if it's not a category that you're already paying for, do not add the hack to your list. You're not trying to increase the things you pay for just because it "sounds good." You must only use the hacks that apply to your current budget, so have that handy!

Sales, Coupons, Discounts and Apps

Sales, coupons, and discounts are truly helpful, but only if they are for items that you would use and are in alignment with your priorities. Every sale is not for you! If seeing the word "sale" is going to trigger you into buying something that is not on your list, then I recommend not receiving emails or using any apps that give discounts or sales.

Price Comparisons

Especially for things like your insurance, it really does pay to shop around, maybe every six months, to see if you can get a discount of any kind! Always start with your current company - but contact other companies to see if a switch may be worth it. This also applies to changing the brand for some of your go-to products.

MLM Parties

An MLM is a multi-level marketing company. An example would be Younique makeup or DoTerra essential oils.

I am *not* telling you to join an MLM to become a marketer or distributor. I *am* saying that often these MLMs have amazing benefits for the host of a party (and bonus, a lot of parties are now online - so no need to clean your house and buy snacks for everyone!). So if you have MLM products that you're going to buy anyway, why not consider throwing a party and see the discounts you can get!

Choose your marketer/distributor wisely! Not all marketers know how to properly throw a party, and therefore, not every party is financially beneficial to the host.

When done properly, the host generally benefits the most from a party, second only to the marketer, and it's a great way to get your necessities on the cheap, or even completely free!

I have five or six main MLMs that I love, and whenever I need to restock, I always start with throwing a party (or sometimes if I don't need a ton of things, I'll just be a guest at someone else's party - often still getting a small discount).

Make sure you do this for stuff you have identified as priorities. For me, books, health and wellness products, cooking spices and a little bit of makeup are my top items. And I definitely have brand loyalty towards these companies.

MLMs fall into a priority for me on multiple categories.

Affiliate Marketing

This is essentially where you recommend your favorite products to others, usually via a special link associated with you in some way. When people purchase something when using your link, you either get a deposit into your PayPal or bank account, or sometimes an amazing discount on your next order.

And bonus, the customer doesn't pay anything extra for using your link. They pay what they would without the link, and you get a small cut. The best ones provide a credit or cash to you AND a credit to the new customer you introduced to the company. A win-win.
Again, only use for products that you love, and be mindful of not promoting random items, just because it's a great deal. Focus on what will either reduce your expenses or create an income for you.

When I lived in a permanent home (vice full-time traveling), I was most successful with Stitch Fix, and ButcherBox - I literally never ordered from either company without using some type of affiliate discounts. Another one would be my Amazon affiliate links like this one, which is my favorite luggage: https://amzn.to/2xWiDiV.

Now that I'm traveling, my greatest affiliate link is for Airbnb which I have used exclusively in my travels abroad so far, which is pretty cool. The affiliate link pays for part (or theoretically all, although I haven't hit that sweet spot yet) of my rent while also giving my friends a discount on their first rental! Here's my link if you've never tried it: https://www.airbnb.com/c/annh7959?currency=USD.

And I am an affiliate for a single mom traveling community and membership site, which is how I often ensure that the next destination has a community for my son: https://single-moms-do-travel-now.mn.co/share/bkZ3CycRr3OIq9BE?utm_source=manual.

So again, look at the products you are already purchasing: Is there a way to contact the company for discounts, or an affiliate link? No harm in trying!

Which hacks are you going to try?

Respecting Income Sources

Sometimes we don't give enough credit to the companies we work for, or our current jobs. Maybe you hate your job or the people you work with, it's draining the life out of you and it's hard to appreciate why you're even going to work every, single day.

Let's find three reasons why this job matters and how it is benefitting you.

First, it's an income source, which is the primary reason why you took the job, whether you still love it or not. It is because of this income that you can start (if you haven't already) building the life of your dreams, the life that's in alignment with your priorities, your purpose. So if nothing else, this is the stepping stone you're using to get where you need to go.

The second is that your job may come with benefits that you sometimes dismiss. It may be providing your medical and dental insurance, or allowing you to invest in a 401K, stocks or other retirement accounts. Perhaps you get some sort of payment for vacation days, sick days, and even things like maternity or paternity leave (although these are never long enough).

Let yourself appreciate the fact that in addition to your paycheck, you are getting these benefits as well.

And last but not least, this job may be providing opportunities for growth, either within the company itself, like a promotion or an increase in pay, or outside the company by getting the experience and skills to land another job that is more aligned with your priorities.

Just by having this income you can put your finances to work towards your priorities, even if the job itself is not ideal. There are always opportunities for growth.

You want to show respect and gratitude by taking full advantage of these positives!

Put the income you make towards your priorities (using the recommendations in this book), take advantage of medical/dental benefits by getting seen by the doctor as needed, invest into the company stock programs ESPECIALLY if there's any type of matching provided! (Seriously, there are very few investments that will double your investment, but stock matching means that for every stock you purchase, the company gives you a stock for free! Heck yeah!). And don't forget to enjoy those vacation days - take whatever "me" time you are able to, even if it's also on the days that your child is sick and unable to go to daycare or you're using that time finding a job you will enjoy more!

This doesn't mean that you cannot or shouldn't quit, or look for another job to replace this one. I'm just saying there's a true benefit to appreciating what your current job does for you rather than constantly focusing on the negative.

And yes, there are some jobs that are literally a waste of your time and the "benefits" do not help your situation at all. In this case run, don't walk, towards another job or income source!

But if you see a benefit to the job, if you would be devastated to be fired tomorrow, then make sure that you are, at a minimum, a useful asset for the company. If you are lucky enough to love this job: become irreplaceable.

I will note that becoming "irreplaceable" is a concept: we're all replaceable. From the CEO down. Every one of us. But sometimes our supervisors don't know that, so let them believe it.

I also do not mean that I think you should become a workhorse, doing "all the things" for "all the people." Focus on doing your thing, the thing that provides amazing value to your company, and also allows you to improve exponentially.

Often if you are "irreplaceable" you're actually given more freedoms to change the culture of the company positively, or the freedom to be more of an essentialist at work, so you can spend your time focusing on your other priorities and of course, more opportunities for advancement and pay increases.

The book, Essentialism, by Greg McKeown really covers the concept very well. I found it life-changing in multiple ways. And as a bonus, I got out of like 90% of the meetings I used to attend, while still maintaining my highest efficiency ratings. It was ridiculously awesome.

Never be the "bare minimum" employee. This employee is literally wasting their time, not making any improvements, burning bridges, which will decrease the likelihood of finding and keeping their dream job. It will increase the likelihood of either getting fired, or at least not receiving any pay increases. You're not here to waste anybody's time, least of all yours. Keep your motivation high for improving and learning. Keep your eyes peeled for amazing opportunities. Always.

Speaking of amazing opportunities, is the FACT that we all need multiple sources of income. Whether they are passive or active, this world is too unpredictable (world-wide quarantine, anyone?) to assume that any one income source is ever rock-solid.
So having a secondary source of income, even if it's not significant enough to fully sustain your lifestyle, is a must.

I would like to mention that while your J.O.B. might not be your ideal occupation, I would HIGHLY recommend that you focus on your passions and things you enjoy doing when it comes to any secondary income. While yes, tough times call for tough decisions and it may not always be possible to have even a secondary job that you enjoy, make sure those moments are temporary. ALWAYS keep your eyes open for opportunities that you will actually ENJOY and start there.

Secondary Income Sources:

Why do I (and every reputable person who covers having a budget) keep stressing multiple income sources? Is it because every millionaire usually has from 7 to 12 income sources?

No. Because becoming a millionaire may not be your priority.

It's because we know having all your eggs in one basket is a huge risk. Baskets and jobs disappear every day.

Just as you would want your investments to be diversified, so also you should diversify your income sources.

In this way, if one income source decreases or gets eliminated entirely, you aren't in the awful position of having to make up for a 100% loss.

Or, better yet, if you hate a particular income source (which might be your greatest income source), then you can start strategizing how to rely less on that source, because you have other sources to rely on instead.

Today your income source may 100% be your 9 to 5 job. Which means, whether you love or hate that job, it is a necessary fact in your life and you're less likely to risk quitting in order to take on another opportunity.

But what if your 9 to 5 was only 70% of your income? It would be less risky changing that 9 to 5 for a better opportunity, wouldn't it?

While focusing on how to prioritize where your money goes is a valid and necessary task, also keep in mind that prioritizing your time, and having diversity of income is equally important. Sometimes you may be living paycheck to paycheck, NOT because of your poor spending choices, but because you legitimately need to get paid more!

While all of these concepts may not appeal to you now, take time to at least consider what these sources of income would mean for you, not just your finances, but for your time as well. Time, whether you like it or not, is always worth more than your money. So you need to make sure that your incomes also line up with your priorities.

So let's look at some ways to increase or diversify your income sources!

Remember, this doesn't mean having seven jobs, just seven income sources. Here's a list of some secondary income sources for inspiration.

Earned Income: This is a more "traditional" concept. Literally, it's having a second job, trading time for money.

But Earned Income doesn't have to be getting a traditional job! There are also *scheduled jobs* where, at zero risk of losing the income source, you can change your schedule about two weeks in advance. Teaching English online is often this way. You create a schedule two weeks in advance, and are expected to keep it, but you could easily change your hours dramatically the following two weeks (rather than having an employer who demands 20 hours a week, or will only let you work on the weekends, etc). There are some online customer service jobs that may do this also.

You can get a time-flexible part-time job where you create your own hours completely and have the luxury to change your hours on a whim without punishment. This would be things like becoming an Uber driver, or one of the delivery companies (like Uber Eats, Shipt, Instacart, etc.), or becoming a captioner/transcriber on Rev.

Ask yourself this: what are you already doing with your "free" time? Is there a way to take a hobby or activity that you're already doing and turn it into an income? To be honest, one of the most appealing parts of becoming a video captioner is the fact that I found myself watching a lot of YouTube videos during my spare time. It occurred to me that I could be getting paid to do this if I just added transcribing to the mix.

You could also seek a positional advancement with a raise at your current job. This advancement may or may not come with additional working hours depending on the industry or company.

Business Income: Ever consider starting your own business?

If this idea seems daunting, remember that this includes things like becoming an Etsy seller, opening a bakery from your kitchen, a babysitting service, starting a blog or YouTube channel, selling your amazing photography skills, teaching others to do what we do, become an author or creating print-on-demand shirts and selling them on Amazon or RedBubble.

At this point, I am NOT suggesting starting an official business. Dip your toe in, see if you like it, love it, if it's sustainable.

You have plenty of time later to form an official LLC or S Corp if your idea becomes profitable. But for now, test the waters out and see what's possible.

That being said, if and when you do decide to start an official business, I highly recommend finding a mentor that aligns with your values.

Mentors I have learned from and recommend:

Chalene Johnson's Marketing Impact Academy (Chalene has been in the business of mentoring entrepreneurs and teaches from A to Z, with a more independent, slow and steady pace.)

Nicole Walters' $1K in 1 Day Academy (Huge on community and networking, Nicole quickly teaches three main ways to build a business. And bonus, her husband is a small business attorney!)

Chanel Morales' Dream Club (Want to learn directly from a traveling single mother? Chanel Morales lives to help other single mothers start their location-independent careers. She is also very community-driven as well.)

My number one rule for mentors, however, is to always trust your gut. We all learn in such different ways, that not everyone will be a perfect fit.

Interest Income: This is income created from lending your money out.

This could be as simple as earning interest in a high-yield savings account, a certified deposit, or participating in P2P lending (peer-to-peer lending such as Lending Club or Funding Circle), or real-estate crowd-funding.

Dividend Income: This is money that's distributed from owning shares of stock in a company.

If you go this route, highly recommend looking up Dividend Aristocrats for a list of dividend-stable companies, while also mixing with some newer, yet reliable companies.

Rental Income: This could be renting a home, a car, a bicycle, you name it. There are even people who rent out their purses!

Capital Gains Income: This comes from selling something and making a profit.

Most commonly this could include the sale of real estate, various arts, or stocks.

Royalties and Licensing Income: This is similar to creating your own company, but rather you create a product, idea or process and you get paid when others use it. There are those that consider print-on-demand selling to be a part of this as well.

Keep in mind that if anything is sold as a get-rich-quick scenario, there's a problem. You should do a TON of research into each opportunity! It is extraordinarily rare that any of these income sources could make you "rich quickly." Even if you have some success early on, for long-term success, you're going to want to continue learning more and more about the field.

Unlike a traditional earned income source, there are income opportunities that could lead to financial losses! Make sure you know what you are getting into!

Start with adding one new income source at a time, so you have time to learn more about that income source and how to make the most of it before moving onto the next source. We don't want to spread ourselves too thin! And ALWAYS find a mentor. The mentor could be as simple as a YouTuber or author that teaches on the topic, or a person you know who can provide insight. Always start with free resources before you pay a mentor, especially to see if you are even able to learn from a particular mentor's teaching style! Just because one person is "known" to be amazing, doesn't mean they will be amazing for you. Go with your gut.

The Emergency Fund

I had a friend who asked me how much money she should be putting aside for her savings, especially because she was a single mother, had significant debts, and other financial obligations. I told her my policy (which is somewhere between $500 to $2,000) and some of my reasoning behind it, and she informed me that she had $1500 already set aside, but she just wasn't sure if it was enough.

Based on our discussions, I told her that it was a great amount and she should start focusing on other priorities and to not add more to her emergency fund at this time.

Well, of course, anything you are working on will quickly come under attack, and her washing machine broke later that week. She called me in a panic: "What do I do? I can't afford this in my budget, but we HAVE to have clean clothes! I need help!"

I asked whether she still had the $1500 sitting there for an emergency. She confirmed that she did.

It took her a minute to realize THIS was the purpose of her savings. This was a prime moment where she could, worst-case-scenario, replace the entire washing machine if needed because she did have the money. We talked and she ultimately decided to see if someone could come and repair her machine, rather than getting a new or used one. So the $50 or so dollars that it cost to repair her machine, which she did not have in her budget this pay period, was taken out of her emergency fund. The machine was repaired, and the catastrophe was downgraded to an inconvenience.

The next pay period, she took her "extra money" and applied the first $50 towards her savings to replenish it back to $1500, and then went on as usual, focusing on her other priorities.

But what if her emergency had cost more than what she had in her savings?
Worst-case scenario, she would have to go into some debt. But not as much debt as if she had zero in her emergency fund.

But also, depending on the emergency, using your emergency fund or going into debt aren't the only options available. Some emergencies have time to be rectified; they don't all need to be handled immediately, even a broken washing machine. Laundromats can be super time-consuming, but it's also temporarily more affordable if it's not in your budget or savings to replace or repair.

So let's discuss having an emergency fund.

Generally speaking, $2,000 is a comfortable amount and it should be in a simple savings account. It makes the funds more liquid or easy to cash or transfer when it's in a savings account, so you can take care of emergencies quickly.

But what if you've never saved even $500 before? What if money in your savings account, much like cash, will slip through your fingers and you just know that you can never save up even $500?

Story Time: It may surprise you but that was me. By the time I was 22, I had accumulated $22,000 in credit card debt. And not just on one credit card. I had about 20 different store cards plus the major cards. You read that correctly: *store cards.* I went $22,000 in debt on eating out, going to the movies, and buying books, movies, clothes, gifts and knickknacks. Not even a car to show for it. Everything was an "emergency". If I was having a bad day, I needed to go shopping to feel better. Saving money was pointless because I would keep having these "emergencies" and I would spend anything I had saved.

It was at my first duty station in the Navy that my work center supervisor, ET2 Jones, realized I had a problem. That I had no idea how to "adult" when it came to my finances.

He was the first person who taught me to "pay myself first" and have money put aside for emergencies and the future. He was NOT the first to attempt to teach me these concepts. The Navy teaches these concepts on repeat and I had probably heard this at least three times prior. But he was the first one to have a one-on-one with me, and the first one I truly HEARD.

I told him that there was no way I had the willpower to just let money "sit there", so he gave me another alternative: to open a CD (certified deposit) at my bank. He forced me to save $200 (which at the time was the minimum initial deposit into a CD at my bank, you can find lower amounts now) and literally had me do this by (gasp) skipping one month of minimum payments on one of my numerous credit cards and then budgeting a mere $10 a month that would go into this CD.

And then he told me the repercussions of cashing out the CD was financial suicide and I would ultimately lose it all if I even attempted it. Now my financial literacy was, at this point, pretty low as you can imagine, so I simply let myself believe him. I mean, I was already putting a LOT of faith into his crazy notions of paying myself first and skipping payments.

And while a CD is not as liquid as a savings account, it is still fairly liquid and not the financial suicide that he led me to believe. I give him props for finding a way to make me save.

And saving that $10 a month? It was the most mentally painful thing I had ever done! Seriously, every time I saw that $10 disappear into my CD, it hurt my heart thinking of the knickknacks and randomness that money could have purchased.

A year later (it was a one year CD), I had a whopping $320 in this account! (You're reading that correctly, CDs, much like a savings account, makes almost zero interest.)

And while this seems like a small number now, I had NEVER saved $320 in my life! And by the end of that year, saving $10 a month was easy! I was kicking myself in the butt for not increasing that $10 to something higher and immediately bumped it up to $50 a month, and before the next year was over it was $200 a month.

ET2 Jones had created in me, the ability to save. And it was AMAZING!

So just know that you can save the $500 in many ways and while, yes, speed is of the essence, if you're a stubborn student like I can be, it's okay if it takes you a year to do this.

The point is to start putting money aside. And if you need it to be a little more difficult to cash out, put it into a CD.

So if you haven't created a policy on how and how much to put into an emergency fund, let's do it now.

First, let's go ahead and revisit your priorities once again. You'll learn that any time you create policies in your life, you're going to measure them against your plumb line, which is your priorities.

Remember that policies aren't just random "good ideas." There are guidelines that must be met.

1. They must not, in any way, shape or form, harm any of your priorities.
2. They must directly support at least one priority.
3. Less is more, you do not need everything to be spelled out in a policy.

So what have you decided? Will your policy have you saving $500 or going for that $2000? Will you be able to leave it in a savings account or something more secure like a CD?

I've had students ask if they should increase it above $2,000 if they have a large family. And the answer is, sure! Of course you could save more. If you have a large family of 10, then it may make sense to bump it up to $5,000. But I will let you know now that this is NOT the only savings you will have. So there's no need to over stress this amount.

A sample emergency savings policy could be stated as:

"I will keep $1,000 in my savings account for emergencies, and another $1,000 in a CD. This will prevent going into debt over a small emergency, and will help me to feel at peace with my budgeting every time I see that I still have the $2,000 in total saved."

Ready for a budget?

Alright, we are more than halfway through this book on finances, and have yet to actually get into the making of a budget. Does that strike you as odd?

Let's get real. In my first draft of this book, as well as in the course I taught, creating a budget was one of the first things we did. And in a classroom environment that translated fairly well because I could go through the budget individually with my students.

Actually, scratch that. If I were being honest, it didn't translate that well in the classroom environment, either. It's WHY I had to go through and help students individually with their budget. We created it too quickly in the course.

It wasted our time.

If you were to have created a budget prior to this moment, and especially if you tried creating one before we delved into making sure your expenses and bills were in alignment with your priorities, you would, just as my students initially did, automatically add in all the things you are used to paying for without discernment! And once you spend time adding them into your budget, it turns out that you are more resistant to changing them up.

It's literally setting you up for failure by having you creating your budget before you fully understand whether something even belongs IN your budget.

So in answer to the question: Are we ready for a budget yet?

The answer is finally... sort of.

Because I'm going to share a secret with you that no financial coach ever wants to say because it's crazy illogical. You don't actually NEED to follow a budget.

There.

I said it.

Now don't get me wrong: I am a budgeter, and I believe that everyone needs at least a framework to spring from.

If you don't know ANYTHING about your budget, then I recommend you create one.

And I additionally recommend that you at least create one "periodically"... every pay period or month is common, but there's nothing wrong with making a budget every two, three, even six months or a year. Plenty of people survive without ever sitting down to actually write out a budget.

But I would add that of the non-budgeters who are financially thriving: They KNOW how to make more than they spend, OR they know how to make money spontaneously. They know how to crowd-source, how to sell, how to provide a needed service.

The non-budgeters who are financially thriving: They KNOW how to put money aside for a rainy day. They KNOW that they are okay because periodically they check their financial pulse to make sure everything is running as it should.

And at least half trust a bookkeeper, accountant or financial management service that will let them know when something is not according to plan.

The next three chapters cover how I recommend people make a budget, which is really just a plan for your money.

You can choose to be SUPER detail-oriented and budget to the penny... or you can be super lax and just keep a concept around.

You can consolidate your bank statements daily, weekly, monthly... Or you can choose to consolidate your bank statements just in time for taxes.

You can create one via a spreadsheet or with a pencil and paper.

It's honestly up to you, your personal style. Don't let the making or oversight of a budget scare you. It's just your plan and it can change as often as you like. Much like writing down your priorities. It's just a plan for where you want to be.

Make sure that every time you swipe your card, every time you notice a penny leaving your bank account, every time you commit to a subscription service... that it's ALL in alignment with your priorities and policies AND the outline of your budget.

Okay. We are finally to the point where we can start creating your budget.

The Priority-Focused Budget (By Pay period)

In this chapter you're going to make sure that *every line item* of your budget and your investments is in accordance with those priorities you've written out. Stop putting money towards things that are not a priority!

You've written down what your current situation is during the pre-work assignments. Now you're going to write out the budget you're going to follow this pay period (or the next pay period if it's close). Yes, you will be making a budget by pay-period. And while most pay periods have a lot of similarities, no two pay periods are identical.

First determine what your most reliable pay periods look like. This may be monthly, bi-monthly, weekly, etc. (In rare occasions it may actually be quarterly or even annually!) Then you will create a budget for each pay period.

For example, if you get paid once a month, then you'll have one budget per month (12 budgets a year). If you get paid twice a month, you'll end up with a set of two budgets, (or 24 budgets in a year), and so on and so forth.

What expenses will come specifically out of that pay period? For each pay period, you're going to figure out what your income amount is, subtract the minimum payments due to debts during that pay period, subtract the bills due in that pay period, and subtract the flexible expenses expected in that pay period. As you create your budget, take time to make sure that EVERY bill you write down, EVERY expense, is part of your priorities. You will no longer be paying for things that don't serve you.

Anything you aren't happy, excited, grateful, honored, thrilled, ecstatic, and grateful to purchase or spend your money on, should be reconsidered.

This will hopefully leave you with a balance that you will put towards your investments, which is the second part of your budget, your investments. We will delve deeper into investments through the next chapters, so for now we will focus on investing into your emergency fund which you created a policy for in the last chapter.

The formula should look like this:

Budget for this pay period:

Your total Income for this pay period
minus Minimum Payments towards your debts during this pay period
minus Obligatory Bills for the pay period
minus Flexible Expenses for the pay period.
_____

What is left over will become your Investment Budget, which at this point is only your emergency fund. So everything remaining will go towards your emergency fund.
_____

With nothing remaining.

The Pay-Yourself-First Method

I pondered deleting this chapter entirely as it can sometimes cause confusion. But the pay-yourself-first budget, while mathematically the same as the full budget method learned in chapter 8, switches the order of things just enough to emphasize your financial investments over your daily budget.

So we will simply re-write the budget as:

Budget for this pay period:

Your total Income for this pay period
minus a firmly set amount that you will put into your Emergency savings account
minus Minimum Payments towards your debts during this pay period
minus Obligatory Bills for the pay period
minus Flexible Expenses for the pay period.
_____

With nothing remaining (and on the off-chance that anything is remaining, you would put the balance into your Emergency savings account).

Do you see what we did there?

We simply pushed your savings requirements as the first thing we focused on after getting paid.
This is often called the pay-yourself-first budget method because

you start with your investment priorities first, and then budget the rest towards life expenses.

What's the benefit?

Rather than thinking of your emergency minimum as what's "left over" after your pay period budget, we make it your first priority.
So in this way, you determine an amount that you have decided you must put towards your emergency fund first - and as soon as you get paid, you immediately move that money into this account.

Then you pay the minimums on your debts, then those obligatory bills, and then, with the "flexible expenses"... you simply make it work!

We're tying back into one of my favorite sayings: Necessity is the mother of invention.

You're basically pretending that you don't have more money when you go to deal with those flexible expenses, and it forces your mind to "figure it out." Perhaps it will encourage you to double check your obligatory payments: to double check if you can get cheaper insurance, if you really need a land line, if you're wasting money with a gym membership when you could find cheaper or free options.

Again, this is mathematically the exact same budget as before. Nothing has changed but how you perceive the budget.

It's a great tool to get you to focus on your financial priorities!

Irregular or Insufficient Pay Periods

Budgeting by your most reliable pay periods may be a little more complicated for some than others, depending on if you have inconsistent or insufficient pay periods.

So how does this really look?

Well, if you get paid monthly, it's fairly easy as a lot of our obligatory expenses tend to work in monthly cycles.

Monthly Income

minus Minimum Payments of every debt

minus Obligatory Bills of every bill

minus Flexible Expenses of every bill

_____

putting the remainder into your emergency fund.

_____

Zero left over.

But let's say you get paid twice a month (as I did when I was in the military).

Then it would look more like this:

First-of-the-month Income

minus Minimum payments of debts due during this period

minus Obligatory bills that are due during this period

minus Flexible expenses that are due during this period

_____

putting the remainder into the emergency fund

_____

Zero left.

15th-of-the-month Income

minus Minimum payments of debts due during this period

minus Obligatory bills that are due during this period

minus Flexible expenses that are due during this period

_____

putting the remainder into the emergency fund

_____

Zero left.

But what if the majority of your debts and your obligatory bills are all due in the first month? Now if your income can cover it all in one pay period - awesome! But if it cannot, especially for your larger bills such as the rent/mortgage, what can you do?

Well, there are two options (and sometimes it's not your choice, but the choice of the creditor or whomever you owe).

Option 1: Create a "budget carryover" on the 15th-of-the-month income. Let's say you're short $500 on the first-of-the-month pay period in this example. You would essentially save $500 of the second pay period, to go towards the next month's budget. This may be difficult initially so prior planning is mandatory!

So then it would look like this:

First-of-the-month Income PLUS "$500 budget carryover" from the last pay period
minus Minimum payments of debts due during this period
minus Obligatory bills that are due during this period
minus Flexible expenses that are due during this period
_____

(You will most likely not do anything with investments at this point)
_____

Zero left.

15th-of-the-month Income

minus Minimum payments of debts due during this period

minus Obligatory bills that are due during this period

minus Flexible expenses that are due during this period

minus $500 "budget carryover" for the next pay period

_____

putting the remainder into the emergency fund

_____

Zero left.

Option 2: Talk to your creditors and see if there's a way for you to split the expenses, or change the payment due dates.

In this example, you might contact your credit cards, your cell phone company, and other companies you have bills for and ask whether, instead of making payments on the first of the month, you could simply make payments on the 16th of the month, thereby "balancing out" the two budgets.

I've had some apartment complexes that were willing to also split my rent into two payments (they wanted me to pay the first "half" up front, that way by the first of the month, I would have paid a full month) and my mortgages have always worked with me on this as well, often without the need to pay anything in advance (this is different from making bi-weekly payments).

Often the most "unmovable" are the utilities, such as electric or house gas, but I would still call and see if they're willing to be flexible.

Start by calling to address your biggest expenses and working your way down, as this will have the biggest impact on your budget. So then it would look like this:

First-of-the-month Income

minus Minimum payments of debts during this period (eg. one credit card)

minus Obligatory bills that are due during this period (eg. all of rent and utilities)

minus Flexible expenses that are due during this period

_____

Nothing towards investments

_____

Zero left.

15th-of-the-month Income

minus Minimum payments of debts due during this period (eg. car payment and a credit card)

minus Obligatory bills that are due during this period (eg. cell phone bill and Netflix)

minus Flexible expenses that are due during this period

_____

putting the remainder into the emergency fund

_____

Zero left.

But what if your pay periods are really wonky?

For example, maybe you get paid an inconsistent amount every week, or some of your income sources are seasonal.

Generally speaking, one of two scenarios will exist.

In the first scenario, you will need to create a special savings account for your future expenses. This is separate from your emergency fund as this is not an emergency. It is a known situation.

Example: you get paid $8,000 but it only happens every three months.

When you get paid, pay the expenses for the current month (which, as an example, might be $2,500). Then save $5,000 for the next two months in a special account, assuming that those months' expenses are also $2,500 (remember that each month may have different expenses), and put the remainder towards your Investment Budget ($500 into your emergency minimum).

Month one:

Get paid $8,000

minus Minimum payments of every debt for month one

minus Obligatory bills of every bill for month one

minus Flexible expenses of every bill for month one

minus $5,000 in savings (the expected budget for the next two months)

_____

minus $500 Emergency minimum

_____

Zero left.

Month two:

Take one month's worth ($2,500) out of savings

minus Minimum payments of every debt for month one

minus Obligatory bills of every bill for month one

minus Flexible expenses of every bill for month one

_____

Zero left (you already put your investment budget into its category last month)

Month three:

Take the remaining month's worth ($2,500) out of savings

minus Minimum payments of every debt for month one

minus Obligatory bills of every bill for month one

minus Flexible expenses of every bill for month one

_____

Zero left (you already put your investment budget into its category last month)

In another scenario, maybe one income source is significantly larger with another income source that is dramatically smaller and paid at different frequencies.

So for this example, let's say you get a monthly amount of $2,000 from your primary job, and a weekly amount that ranges between $150 and $200 from a side job.

A possible breakdown is to divide the expenses so that the $150/week is responsible for a certain type of expense, while the rest is covered by the $2,000. And anything you get over the $150/week (or anything that you didn't need of the $150) gets thrown into your investment budget or a pre-planned purpose or priority.

So for this example:

First-of-the-month Income is $2,000

minus Minimum payments of debts during this period

minus Obligatory bills that are due during this period (eg. all of rent and utilities)

minus Flexible expenses that are due during this period (with the exception of groceries and eating out)

_____

putting the remainder into the emergency fund

_____

Zero left.

First Weekly Income $150

minus $150 Groceries and eating out for the week

_____

Zero left.

Second Weekly Income $175

minus $150 Groceries and eating out for the week

_____

minus $25 emergency minimum

_____

Zero left.

And so on.

The difficulty comes, of course, if your payments are so irregular and/or are not enough to easily "save" two months' worth, or whatever the needed duration may be.

Or when, quite frankly, your expenses and bills exceed your income.

This is where you would buckle down and ensure that EVERY line item of expense is within your priorities (and maybe even temporarily less than your priorities, but within living requirements). You would contact each of your bills' creditors and see if you can reduce them in any way, until you can have this additional savings account to float each pay period. You may even consider selling things that are not a priority (or not a right-now priority), downsizing your home, moving in with family, etc.

This is also where you start to look at your income sources and see how to increase them. While it's not always easy, living paycheck-to-paycheck is clearly unsustainable, and difficult decisions will need to be made.

To be fair, we should always be looking at ways to increase our income. Cost of living inflation is a thing, and unfortunately, many industries do not provide increases in pay in accordance with the cost of living changes. If you are living anywhere near the paycheck-to-paycheck level, increasing your income should be a major focus.

Okay, enough with budgets, let's get on with our investments.

The Debts

There is only one real rule to paying off your debts: pay off one debt at a time.

I made the mistake of attempting to pay off multiple debts at once. When I had my 20-some credit card debt—insert face palm emoji here—I thought I would pay every card "a little extra" rather than focusing all my effort on one debt. Little did I realize that this was the slowest possible method I could have chosen. I again want to thank ET2 Jones for teaching me this simple, but crazy effective method! He was firm in believing that after I put aside some money for emergency, I need to tackle one debt at a time.

So while you should pay the minimum payment on ALL of your debts on time, anything extra that you have, should immediately go into one, designated debt (assuming you have multiple debts).

The debt snowball concept has been around forever but Dave Ramsey definitely made it popular.

The basics of debt snowball is to list your debts from the lowest balance to the highest, and to pay off the lowest balance first, and work your way up to the highest balance. Once a debt is paid off, the amount you were previously putting towards that debt should immediately be put towards the next debt you are tackling.

For example:

Debt 1 minimum payment is $200.
Debt 2 minimum payment is $400.

You are currently paying an extra $100 towards debt 1, meaning you have a total of $300 going towards debt 1 each month.

Once debt 1 is fully paid off, that $300 should now go towards debt 2, in addition to the $400 you were already paying for the minimum payment. You should now be paying $700 towards debt 2.

Don't decrease this amount unless you are, with serious decision-making, adding another obligation somewhere else (like maybe you're going to start sending your son to piano lessons once debt 1 is paid off).

But as a general, wait on the piano lessons until all your debts are paid off.

In this way you can get faster "wins." You can pay off a smaller debt faster, thereby making you feel like you've won faster than if you were to tackle a larger balance first.

If you're able to completely pay off a debt in one pay period, do so. No need to keep any debt around that you can easily pay off.

If you can pay off multiple debts in that same pay period, again, you should do so.

But for any debts that will take more than a pay period to pay off, you may use one of four methods.

1. **Pay off the lowest balance first**. (Psychologically VERY satisfying and is one of the most popular methods)
2. **Pay off the highest interest rate first**. (Mathematically it makes sense to focus on interest rate, but studies have shown that we're talking about a VERY small monetary win, compared to what can be a HUGELY stressful method when compared to paying the lowest balance first).
3. **Pay off the most stressful or annoying debts first**. (This is where you may choose to pay off debts to friends and family first, or to prioritize getting rid of joint debts with a former spouse or partner.)
4. **Pay off loans before credit cards**. (This is a method referred amongst shopaholics as it is generally harder to get a loan than it is to use a credit card. So if you pay off a credit card first, you could easily just use that credit card the next day and go back into debt. If you pay off a loan first, generally you'll have to get a new loan in order to go further into debt, which may not be worth the hassle for you.)

One thing to strongly consider: If you have a debt (credit card or a loan) where the interest rate is temporarily zero or super low for a certain amount of months, you would generally want to prioritize this debt above others to not only take advantage of the low interest rate but also because often, if you do not pay the debt off during the promotional months, not only will the interest rate increase drastically for the remaining principal, but often they will actually backdate all the interest that you saved and charge you! This extra interest defeats the purpose of having the zero interest rate in the first place! This is definitely a debt you want to knock out quickly (and well before the promotion ends). If paying this debt off first doesn't make sense, then at least consider your minimum payment to be the amount you should pay each month in order to have the debt completely paid off prior to the promotion end date which is often MUCH higher than the minimum payment the lender recommends.

For example, if your official minimum payment amount is $100 per month, but the total debt is $2,000 with 10 months remaining in the promotion period, you should really be paying at least $200 per month in order to avoid the additional fees.

Other than the promotional interest rate circumstance, the order is honestly almost irrelevant, and you can prioritize it in any way. Each of these methods falls under the "snowball" method, although some refer to paying off the highest interest rate as the "avalanche" method. But when in doubt, paying off the debt with the smallest balance is always my recommendation.

I'll note here that most people do not consider their mortgages to be a true "debt" and will often not pay off their mortgages until much later in their financial maturity, simply because it's often a six-digit number. It's up to you, but I will state that I also lean this route. If you have any six-figure debt (to include college or medical debts) it is reasonable to pay this debt off after some other steps are taken first (and those steps will be discussed in later chapters.)

So again, if you haven't created a policy on how you will pay off your debts, let's do it now.

But first, as always, let's go ahead and revisit your priorities once again. Any time you create policies in your life, you're going to measure them against your plumb line, which is your priorities.

Remember that policies aren't just random "good ideas." There are guidelines that must be met.

1. They must not, in any way, shape or form, harm any of your priorities.
2. They must directly support at least one priority.
3. Less is more, you do not need everything to be spelled out in a policy.

So what have you decided? Which debts will you pay off first? Will you add your mortgage or other six-figure debts, if you have any, to this list or save it for a later time?

A sample debt-snowball policy could be stated as:

"So long as my emergency fund is still at $2,000 (or whatever amount you have decided), and after all my minimum payments have been made on all my debts, I will put at least $200 above the minimum payment towards my car payment until it is paid off, and then use the snowball method to pay off my next smallest debt and so on. I will enjoy not having a car payment until I am completely debt free!"

I hope you can see by the verbiage of the sample debt-snowball policy, that you will never focus on your debts if you don't have your pre-determined emergency fund solid. There's no point paying off your debts if you have nothing at all saved. It means that when there's an emergency, you're going to fall right back into debt. That's just a waste of your time. Stay ahead of the game and have an emergency fund before focusing any energy on your debts.

Your Budget for this pay period may look something like this:

Your total Income for this pay period
minus Minimum Payments towards your debts during this pay period
minus Obligatory Bills for the pay period
minus Flexible Expenses for the pay period.
_____

minus nothing towards emergency fund because it's still at $2,000
minus $200 extra towards car payment
_____

With nothing remaining.

Income Emergency Fund

The income emergency fund is not to be confused with the emergency fund.

The "income emergency fund" is specifically for a full loss of income scenario. This will be enough to cover three to six months of living expenses. That is the ONLY reason for this account and you will not touch this money in any other scenario.

I want to note that I'm using the phrase "loss of income", but this doesn't necessarily mean that you are fired or the company you work for suddenly goes bankrupt or stops paying you.

This could absolutely be used for a time when you need a change in career! It could cover you quitting. This is perfect for those that currently dread going into their 9 to 5, or want to try their hand at a different career entirely.

With the income emergency fund, you could simply choose to leave your job and pursue another! It doesn't have to be a situation where you are covered in case you are fired, although, of course, it does that, too.

At the end of the day, it gives you another choice, in addition to being a safety net.

Have three to six months worth in this fund and as a general rule, the more volatile your situation, the closer to six months you would want. Meaning if you are very likely to be fired, or lose your pay, or to quit, you would want to have closer to six months in the meantime. I'll take this moment to mention that at the time of writing this book, the world is going through the first world-wide pandemic, the coronavirus or COVID-19. There are so many industries and companies that have let go or furloughed their employees that a month prior would have sworn they would never need to resort to such an act. Having an income emergency fund is a must. It's not a recommendation.

How much should you save?

We'll delve into calculating your monthly budget in a later chapter, but there are two methods you could choose to address your income emergency fund. You could literally take the total amount that you normally use each month and multiply by three to six, or you could take the time to calculate how much you really NEED in your budget and multiply this lower number by three to six.

Honestly, I prefer the easier math of just taking your normal, monthly budget and multiplying it by three to six. Yes, in a true emergency you may find yourself saving more and spending less, but in your panic, who knows what you may actually do. Safer to just take your monthly, non-panicked budget, and multiply that by three to six.

Traditionally, an income emergency fund would be put into a simple savings account, much like the regular emergency fund. I certainly wouldn't consider it wrong to do so. But unless you feel that losing your income is imminent, I would actually lean towards putting one week to one month into a savings account (with the highest interest rate you can find), and investing the rest.

My preferences for the income emergency fund is to have one week to one month's worth in a simple savings account, and then rest in any combination of the following:

Roth IRA certified deposits or Roth IRA index funds (this has a limit of $6,000 per year per person, or $7,000 if over the age of 50) and then anything over this amount, or if you are not eligible for an IRA, to put the remainder into a non-IRA certified deposit or index fund.

For certified deposits, shop around for the highest interest rate and dividend rate you can find.

For index funds (or any stock purchasing) you want to find a brokerage who does not charge commission fees. Charles Schwab S&P 500 Index Funds (which you can only purchase through Charles Schwab) or using a service such as M1 Finance which brokers multiple S&P 500 Index Funds.

Why do I recommend as low as a week into a savings account? Because you can do a LOT in a week, and even more with a full month. Generally with a full loss of income, you don't "need" more money until the next time you expected to get paid. Unless that date is tomorrow you should be fine. So having a week or a month's worth readily available should get you through until you are able to cash the rest of your income emergency fund, or able to get additional income.

So again, if you haven't created a policy for your income emergency fund, let's get it done.

But first, you guessed it, let's go ahead and revisit your priorities once again.

Policy guidelines.

1. They must not, in any way, shape or form, harm any of your priorities.
2. They must directly support at least one priority.
3. Less is more, you do not need everything to be spelled out in a policy.

So what have you decided? How many months will you save and how will you calculate a month? Where will it be saved?

A sample income emergency fund policy could be stated as:

"So long as my emergency fund is still at $2,000 (or whatever amount you have decided), and if I am still debt-free with the exception of my mortgage, I will keep six months worth, specifically $12,000 saved. I will put half in a simple savings account, and the other half in a Roth-IRA CD."

I hope you notice by the sample income emergency fund policy, that your first priority when it comes to your investments is to have an emergency fund, THEN to be debt-free (with the exception of your mortgage or six-figure debts) and THEN to focus on your income emergency fund. There really isn't a scenario where you would want to reverse this order.

Your Budget for this pay period may look something like this (notice you are no longer paying your minimums towards debt because you are debt-free!!!):

Your total Income for this pay period
minus Obligatory Bills for the pay period
minus Flexible Expenses for the pay period.
_____

minus nothing towards emergency fund because it's still at $2,000
minus $800 extra towards income emergency savings account.
_____

With nothing remaining.

You Did It!

Alright guys, the last investment policy. By this point, you should be debt free (with the exception of your mortgage or other six-digit debts), and you should have at least 3, if not 6 months in your income emergency fund and $2000 in your emergency fund rather than just $500.

This is a great time, if you haven't done it in a while, to go back to your priorities and possibly tweak them. A lot of time may have passed between then and now, and this is a key milestone period where it really helps to look once again at your priorities. In life, we are always maturing and evolving and you may have different priorities now than you did back then.

This is a much more customizable stage, and I highly encourage you to first complete some research (or perhaps speak to an investment specialist) into the many types of investments that exist including EFTs, mutual funds, traditional vs. Roth IRAs, stocks, bonds, real estate as well as less traditional investments such as starting a business! Honestly the list on ways to invest in your future is practically endless!

In this stage, we will take your investment budget and focus less on your financial priorities, and more on other priorities which perhaps we have been unable to fund until now.

Some possible priorities you may be focusing on, and you may even choose to focus a little on each one, vice focusing on one concept at a time:

1. **Investing in retirement income** (this could be stocks/funds/bonds, real estate, starting or expanding a business to be more autonomous, or anything that you have researched as a viable retirement income source).
2. **Paying off the large debts**: mortgage, large medical debts (six digits), large college debts (six digits).
3. **Putting money aside for other priorities** such as college education for yourself or your children/grandchildren, putting money aside for a down payment on a house, putting money aside for yearly, quarterly, monthly, or weekly traveling. Again, refer to your priorities to see where else you may put your funds.
4. **Putting money aside for giving to charities** (for those that tithe, this would be considered above the amount you tithe normally, which is often part of your daily budget).

The gist: this is an area where you can start to rearrange the entire budget.

Your goal at this stage is to figure out how much you will need coming in each month to continue living comfortably, and continue building a system of incomes, as discussed in chapter 5 to ensure you can have that income, with a strong emphasis on passive income. The fact is, at this point, your current income IS enough to sustain you, especially as you have no debt and you already have your emergency and income emergency money set aside.

What you need to focus on, however, is how you can PASSIVELY maintain that same income amount (or higher because you never know how long you will be able, or how long you will want to continue working). Will you be able to quit your 9 to 5, if you haven't already, and still have enough coming in to maintain your lifestyle?

The more volatile your current income sources, the more of your investment budget that should be allocated to increasing passive income. As an example, a traditional job is very volatile - you can be fired any time and there may not be any form of retirement or 401K that you are already investing in, or you may be too young to benefit from those accounts any time soon. An investment specialist will help if you have zero knowledge, but at this stage being investment illiterate can be a very dangerous game. Take the time to learn, from reliable sources, the different ways to invest, what the inherent risks are (investments are, ultimately, gambling) and make sure you steer clear of investment scams.

Once you know a reasonable amount is being set up towards future investments/income sources (many investment specialists will say 15% of your current income should be allocated towards increasing your retirement income), then you can divide the rest into the other priorities mentioned in the very first chapter. To be fair, there's nothing saying you must focus on the investments first - especially if you already have a certain amount of funds, perhaps from a military retirement, already guaranteed every month. But just be realistic about what you will need (and what you will want) in the future.

And you want to know something awesome when it comes to investing? If you use certain investment brokers and apps, they also have... drum roll... referral codes!

What?!? You mean I can make an income from my investments WHILE investing? Yup - and I'm not even talking about dividends here! (And if you don't know about dividends, definitely learn more about that: stocks that pay dividends traditionally give you the most bang for your buck!)
I use M1 Finances and Robinhood as my preferred brokerage of choice and they both offer some sort of referral benefits.

Using my M1 Finance referral code: https://mbsy.co/MWcp9, you and I will both get $10 to invest! And once you have funded your M1 account, you will get your own referral code!

If you prefer Robinhood, then using my referral code: https://join.robinhood.com/annh262, means we will both get a free stock! And again, once you are registered, you will also get a referral code to share. The majority of the free stocks will, of course, be of low value, but I think of it as a better value than buying a lottery ticket.

Another investment app, which I do not personally use, is WeBull which will actually give you two free stocks with a minimum investment of $100 (although that promotion may be going away soon).

Each of these brokerages works differently. I love M1 Finances for allowing me to purchase fractional shares (vice purchasing a whole share at a time) and for letting me create percentage-balances so i don't over-invest in a particular stock or sector of the market; while Robinhood requires a full share purchase, but allows me to name my own price limit so I know I'll never go above my budget amount.

So again, if you haven't created a policy for this last stage of investing, let's get it done.
But first, you already know, let's make sure you know what your priorities are!

Policy guidelines.
1. They must not, in any way, shape or form, harm any of your priorities.
2. They must directly support at least one priority.
3. Less is more, you do not need everything to be spelled out in a policy.
So how will you increase your retirement income at this stage? My hope is that by this point, assuming you were not ready for this point

when you first started reading this book, that you have already increased your retirement income via multiple sources of income! But in case those other methods proved temporary or less passive (meaning you cannot sustain those methods through retirement for some reason), then let's just make sure you've got enough money coming in to support you through retirement! We want to focus on those passive methods at this point.

A sample retirement fund policy could be stated as:

"So long as my emergency fund is still at $2,000, and if I am still debt-free with the exception of my mortgage, with $12,000 saved in my income emergency funds; I will start investing 15% of my income towards the retirement funds recommended by my investment specialist, 10% towards paying off my mortgage, 10% towards quarterly vacations, 10% towards my son's college fund and 10% towards the charities of my choice."

Notice by the sample retirement fund policy, that your first priority when it comes to your investments is to have an emergency fund, to be debt-free, to have a six-month income emergency fund, and then to constantly increase retirement income before focusing on paying off large debts and other priorities.

Frequently Asked Questions

Q: When is bankruptcy/foreclosure/short sale a feasible option?

> A: Bankruptcy is a feasible option when you legitimately cannot make your budget work. You've already gone down to not only your priorities, but to your bare-boned necessities. It is a legal procedure intended for just this purpose. Don't be afraid to do this - but you will definitely need a bankruptcy lawyer to assist.
>
> Foreclosures and short sales are a feasible option when you have a home that is not serving you, and that you cannot sell in the traditional fashion. Never keep or stay in a home that is not serving you.

Q: Should I ever live without medical insurance?

> A: This one is SO tricky. I would state that in the United States, you are carrying the greatest risk if you are without medical insurance of any type. Just a simple ER visit can cost thousands in the blink of an eye. And it goes without saying that if you can't afford insurance, it's highly possible that you also don't have thousands saved for a medical emergency.
>
> The alternative to having medical insurance is to have some type of alternative medical insurance (like a medical share or something similar).

Carrying a high deductible will often reduce medical insurance, but you'll need the cash to pay the deductible or, of course, you could simply have a medical emergency fund.

You would build this up after debts are paid while building your income emergency fund.

But again, medical emergencies can escalate dramatically (in the US especially) so this will be a risk either way.

Q: How about life insurance?

A: This one can be confusing, so let's break it down a bit. The purpose of life insurance is to take care of your loved ones after you pass. There are multiple methods to doing this, but in terms of life insurance, generally you will be looking at term life insurance. Term is infinitely cheaper than whole life insurance and makes more sense since your children really only rely on you during their childhood (let's say until they are at least graduated from high school, but you could also take into account college years.)

Q: But what about your spouse or if your children have permanent medical conditions that would not allow them to take care of themselves even into adulthood?

A: The "ideal" way, is to simply pass on your personal wealth, your savings, your investments and assets onto your spouse and possibly your children, so they can simply carry on with those income sources (hopefully the majority are passive by the time you pass). A reliable trust attorney will be helpful to set things up for you, as each state differs in how this is handled.

If you are, however, concerned that this is insufficient, then you could definitely get whole life insurance. Just know that whole life insurance is infinitely more expensive for each month that you are alive, heavily cutting into your daily budget, especially if you are still at a stage when you are trying to pay off large amounts of debt.

I would say that once you are debt-free and growing your investments, this is where you would strongly consider switching to term life, and connecting with a trust attorney to help you set your legacy to pass onto your spouse or children.

Q: I really want to buy a house. When should I do this?

A: While purchasing a home is something a lot of people dream of doing, remember that the ownership comes at a huge cost! That mortgage plus all the interest, insurance and maintenance/upkeep. Additionally, I'm sure it doesn't surprise you to hear that immediately after purchasing a home, most homeowners will excitedly run to the stores to then furnish and decorate the home, wanting to fill every nook and cranny to make the house feel like home. This is why a better time to purchase your home is after your income emergency fund is met, during the "split priorities" portion of your investments.

This means you are debt free, with plenty in savings, and then you will figure out what type of budget you will have for your mortgage (the principle, interest and insurance), which will lead you to figuring out what type of deposit you will need to pay. Feel free to talk to a real estate agent or banker to figure out if you can apply for a home loan without paying a 20% deposit - but you will still want to have that emergency fund and income emergency fund fully saved - because emergencies abound with homeownership.

Are there exceptions to this?

Yes - there are always exceptions for when you may want to purchase a home, even if you do not have your income emergency fund. But if you can do so with at least your $2000 emergency fund and your other debts paid off, this would be better than buying a home while you still have other debts.

Q: Is the mortgage the only debt that can wait to be paid off until the split priorities step

> A: Generally yes, but an exception could be medical or college debts that are in the six digits as these are also such a large burden, that it may be easiest to focus on these after your income emergency fund is met.

Q: Should I invest in my employer's 401K or other retirement funds even if I'm not debt free or don't have my emergency or income emergency funds maxed out?

> A: Generally, if you are able to meet your daily expenses, and able to contribute something towards your investment budget (so at a minimum, you are able to save something every pay period towards your emergency fund), and you foresee your current job as a long-term investment (it's a job you enjoy and are willing to do for years to come and you have a good work ethic and are unlikely to be fired) then I would, at most, contribute just enough to take the benefits that are sometimes associated with investing into a company's 401K, etc.
>
> Most companies will match up to a certain amount in your investment, and you will want to at least meet that minimum amount.
>
> But don't go over this minimum requirement; no point investing in your retirement when you still have debt. Debts make your retirement life much more burdensome and it is better to get rid of the debt than it is to invest. While a credit card can easily have an interest rate of 20%, it is much more difficult to

guarantee an interest rate of 20% in your investments. So the interest rate alone encourages getting rid of the debt first.

Q: Can I still tithe monthly even if I have debt?

A: This is a question of conviction and priorities. But if tithing is a priority, you would simply add it to your daily budget. You could list it as either an obligatory or flexible expense. I firmly believe that "giving" (not necessarily limited to tithing, but giving in general) may be part of your priority under relationships or even environment, career and health! Again, when something is a priority, you make it work.

But I will also state, that as a general rule - and especially if you are struggling financially - that it's best to make sure there's a certain level of stability in your finances/assets before you give more than what your daily budget allows. Meaning it would be an extreme situation where I would consider giving to fall under a reason to go into debt or to use an emergency fund.

And don't forget, that money is not the only way to give! You can donate physical items that are no longer of use to you, or that you can do without, as well as, the highest gift, which is a donation of your time and services. Again, life is limitless - "giving" does not merely mean to give monetarily.

Wrap Up

So let's wrap this all up!

Here's what I hope you have gained from this book:

You must live your life according to your priorities. YOUR priorities, not anyone else's. Your dreams, your values, your hopes all matter in every decision that you make, but you must first take the time to become clear on what they are.

Once you know what's really important to you, then every decision becomes crystal clear.

And it's no different for your finances.

You can tell what a person values by where they put their money, where they spend their time, and who they surround themselves with.

So take the time to create a schedule for yourself, and for your money.

Your goal is to always have funds to go towards your investment budget. Investing in your future, which is a reflection of your priorities.

Don't get stuck in the mundane part of living paycheck to paycheck. It isn't a way to truly live.

I can't wait to hear about your successes - and even your moments of failure because we honestly learn the most from our failures!

Thank you for the time you took to read this, as there is nothing more precious than your time.

Have any questions for me?

I would love to connect at https://bio.fm/priorityfocusedlife

Recommended Reading

Burchard, Brendon. High Performance Habits: How Extraordinary People Become That Way. Author's Republic. 2019.

Holman, Ann. Priority Focused Finances: Monthly Journal. Independently Published. 2020.

Holman, Ann. Single Mom Travel Adventures: Income. Independently Published. 2020.

McKeown, Greg. Essentialism: The Disciplined Pursuit Of Less. New York: Crown Business. 2014.

Robbins, Mel. The 5 Second Rule. Post Hill Press. 2017.

www.ingramcontent.com/pod-product-compliance
Lightning Source LLC
Chambersburg PA
CBHW070250220526
45465CB00004B/1567